STARTING OUT

DUMP TRUCKS

MEG GREVE

CREATIVE EDUCATION • CREATIVE PAPERBACKS

CONT

ENTS

I SEE A DUMP TRUCK.

Its box rises slowly.

Dirt tumbles out and piles up.

The box is also called a bed.

Dump trucks carry heavy loads.

Dump trucks need help loading up. But they unload all by themselves.

A dump truck was here.

I see deep tire tracks.

Dump trucks are heavy.

A dump truck can hold 28,000 pounds (12,700 kilograms).

I see an old building being torn down.

A new building will go up. Dump trucks carry materials away. They bring materials in.

Out with the old, in with the new.

MAKE A NOISE

BEEP, CR

ASH, SCREECH!

Can you make the sounds of a dump truck?

Listen to these sounds:

https://www.youtube.com/watch?v=HIbdBIAYgc8

Now it is your turn!

DUMP TRUCK WORDS

loads: things that need to be moved

materials: things needed for a job, such as gravel, sand, or dirt

tracks: marks left by a vehicle or another moving thing

unload: to drop off or empty out

READING CORNER

Burton, Jeffrey. *The Wheels on the Dump Truck*. New York: Little Simon, 2020.

Pearson, Peter. *How to Walk a Dump Truck*. New York: HarperCollins, 2019.

Silver, Skye. *Dump Truck Disco*. Concord, Mass.: Barefoot Books, 2021.

INDEX

PUBLISHED BY CREATIVE EDUCATION AND CREATIVE PAPERBACKS
P.O. Box 227, Mankato, Minnesota 56002
Creative Education and Creative Paperbacks are imprints of The Creative Company
www.thecreativecompany.us

LIBRARY OF CONGRESS CATALOGING-IN-PUBLICATION DATA
Title: Dump trucks / by Meg Greve.
Description: Mankato, Minnesota : Creative Education and Creative Paperbacks, [2025] | Series: Starting out | Includes bibliographical references and index. | Audience: Ages 4-7 | Audience: Grades K-1 | Summary: "Dump trucks will introduce budding book learners to a noisy, colorful world with this new Starting Out title. Colorful photos, labeled diagrams, 'Make a Noise' section, glossary, and more ignite a passion for learning"-- Provided by publisher.
Identifiers: LCCN 2023059437 (print) | LCCN 2023059438 (ebook) | ISBN 9798889891710 (library binding) | ISBN 9781682775561 (paperback) | ISBN 9798889891833 (ebook)
Subjects: LCSH: Dump trucks--Juvenile literature. | Construction equipment--Juvenile literature. | CYAC: Dump trucks. | Construction equipment. | LCGFT: Instructional and educational works.
Classification: LCC TL230.15 .G744 2025 (print) | LCC TL230.15 (ebook) | DDC 624.028/4--dc23/eng/20240128
LC record available at https://lccn.loc.gov/2023059437
LC ebook record available at https://lccn.loc.gov/2023059438

DESIGN AND PRODUCTION
Design by Rhea Magaro
Production by Beeline Media and Design
Art direction by Tom Morgan
Printed in the United States of America

PHOTOGRAPHS by Dreamstime (Juri Bizgajmer, Dumitrina Andrusca, Christian Delbert), Getty Images (Martin Diebel, tracielouise), Shutterstock (sutadimages, freestore 839, Sanit Fuangnakhon, RobSt, Gorloff-KV, ericlefrancais, ER_09, Bohbeh, Gargantiopa)